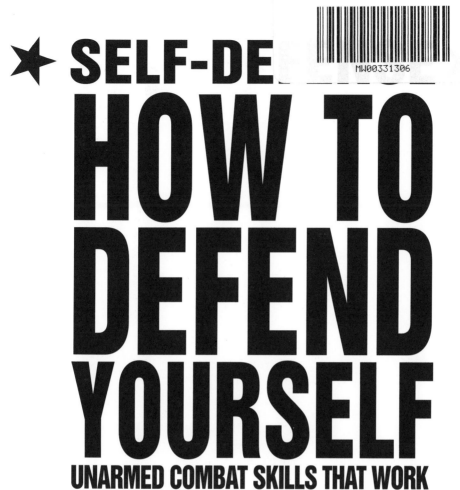

★ SELF-DEFENSE
HOW TO DEFEND YOURSELF

UNARMED COMBAT SKILLS THAT WORK

Martin J. Dougherty

THOMAS DUNNE BOOKS
ST. MARTIN'S GRIFFIN ✌ NEW YORK

THOMAS DUNNE BOOKS
An imprint of St. Martin's Press

Self-Defense: How to Defend Yourself.
Copyright © 2013 by Amber Books Ltd. All rights reserved.
For information, address St. Martin's Press, 175 Fifth Avenue,
New York, N.Y. 10010.

www.stmartins.com

Library of Congress Cataloging-in-Publication Data
on file at the Library of Congress

ISBN: 978-1-250-04195-1 (trade paperback)

Editorial and design by
Amber Books Ltd
Bradley's Close
74–77 White Lion Street
London N1 9PF
United Kingdom
www.amberbooks.co.uk

Project Editor: Michael Spilling
Illustrations: Tony Randell

Printed in China

St. Martin's Griffin books may be purchased for educational,
business, or promotional use. For information on bulk purchases,
please contact Macmillan Corporate and Premium Sales Department at
1-800-221-7945 extension 5442 or write specialmarkets@macmillan.com.

First U.S. Edition

10 9 8 7 6 5 4 3 2 1

PUBLISHER'S NOTE
This book is for information purposes only. Readers should be aware of
the legal position in their country of residence before practicing any of the
techniques described in this book. Neither the author or the publisher can
accept responsibility for any loss, injury, or damage caused as a result of
the use of the combat techniques described in this book, nor for any
prosecutions or proceedings brought or instigated against any person
or body that may result from using these techniques.

Contents

Introduction

Self-defence can be defined as the act of physically resisting an assault or dealing with an assailant. There are various means that can be employed, and different people will prefer to use different methods. There is, strictly speaking, no 'right' or 'wrong' way to defend yourself. There is only what works and what does not. However, a 'successful' defence that lands you in jail is not as big a success as you might have hoped for.

Self-defence is not the same thing as fighting. In a fight, the goal is to defeat the opponent – to make him give up or become physically incapable of continuing. In self-defence the goal is to protect yourself, and that can be quite different.

If you have to knock an assailant out, or render him otherwise incapable of fighting, then that is what you have to do. But not for its own sake: you do it as a means to end the attack. If the attack could be ended by other means – by dissuasion or even flight – then that would be an equally valid method of getting what you want out of the situation.

Good self-defence training is always geared towards protecting you, by various means including but not limited to harming the assailant. It employs simple methods against realistic threats, and includes an understanding of the issues surrounding the use of force. It also addresses the question of what is legal and what is not, and teaches the student to work towards the goal of getting out of a situation while coming to minimal harm.

Layered Defences

Ideally, it is best not to have to 'get physical' with anyone. There can be no legal complications and you cannot get hurt in a fight that does not happen. Physical self-defence should be a last resort when other methods have failed. The fact that you are capable of defeating an assailant does not mean it is worth needlessly putting yourself in harm's way or getting involved in pointless confrontations.

Your first line of defence is to recognize potential threats and stay away from them where possible. We are told from a young age not to take shortcuts down dark alleys and the like, and most of us have ignored this advice at some point. Yet it remains good advice – wherever you can, stay away from places where common sense tells you that you may be vulnerable.

The second line of defence is to be willing to walk away from a situation rather than allow it to become a confrontation. Many physical assaults result from escalation, where two individuals who do not really want to fight anger one another to the point where someone throws a punch. Keeping a cool head and being willing to just go elsewhere can greatly reduce the chances of being involved in violence.

There are, however, some situations where an individual is determined to cause you harm. Your last line of defence before matters become physical is the ability to deter aggression. Most assailants do not want a fight; they want a victim. If the potential assailant can see that you will put up a fight – win or lose – then they may decide that you are not worth the trouble.

The vast majority of situations can be dealt with or avoided altogether by the first three 'layers' of your defences. If violence is imminent and these measures have failed, physical self-defence is the only option remaining.

Realistic Expectations

It is necessary to approach self-defence with realistic expectations. Training is not likely to permit you to defeat 17 people at once, or to take on individuals who are much stronger and heavier than yourself with the certainty of victory. This sort of 'perfect solution' is used as a selling point by some instructors, but the truth is that there is no perfect solution.

Instead we must play the odds and try to obtain the best possible outcome from a given situation. An attack that ends with you hurt is a better outcome than one in which you are killed. A situation where an aggressor calls you all kinds of hurtful things and struts off to tell his friends he 'won' is better than a fight where you knocked him out but were yourself injured.

Training improves your odds of dealing with a given situation, but any fight is going to be a frightening and unpleasant business, and probably painful too. What good self-defence training does is prevent things going from bad to worse. If you need to defend yourself then things are already bad – there's no point in wishing that it wasn't happening. Instead, you must accept a fairly unpleasant reality and deal with it, never forgetting that it's all about you and not the assailant. You win by ending the situation without coming to more harm than necessary. If that is accomplished by taking an opportunity to escape, or by demolishing an opponent, the important part of the outcome is the same.

In short, self-defence is about defending yourself, and not necessarily about harming someone else. Do what you have to, and keep an eye on the goal. That goal, one last time, is to preserve your own safety and wellbeing.

Targets and Vulnerable Points
The main targets of the body include the following areas.

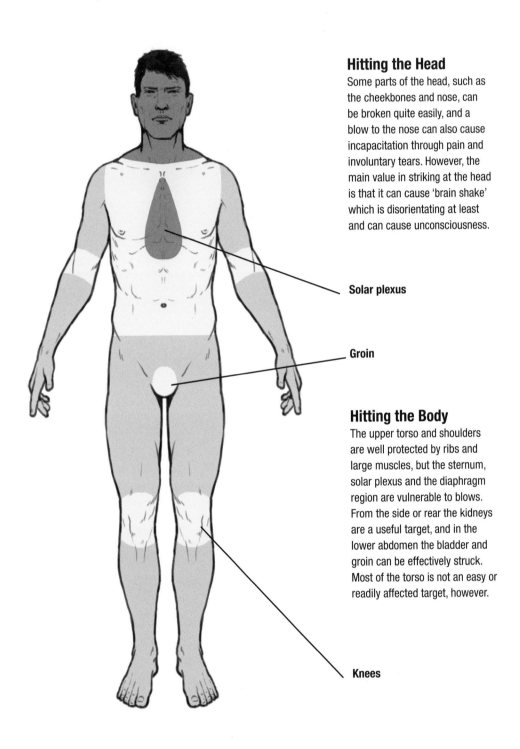

Hitting the Head

Some parts of the head, such as the cheekbones and nose, can be broken quite easily, and a blow to the nose can also cause incapacitation through pain and involuntary tears. However, the main value in striking at the head is that it can cause 'brain shake' which is disorientating at least and can cause unconsciousness.

Solar plexus

Groin

Hitting the Body

The upper torso and shoulders are well protected by ribs and large muscles, but the sternum, solar plexus and the diaphragm region are vulnerable to blows. From the side or rear the kidneys are a useful target, and in the lower abdomen the bladder and groin can be effectively struck. Most of the torso is not an easy or readily affected target, however.

Knees

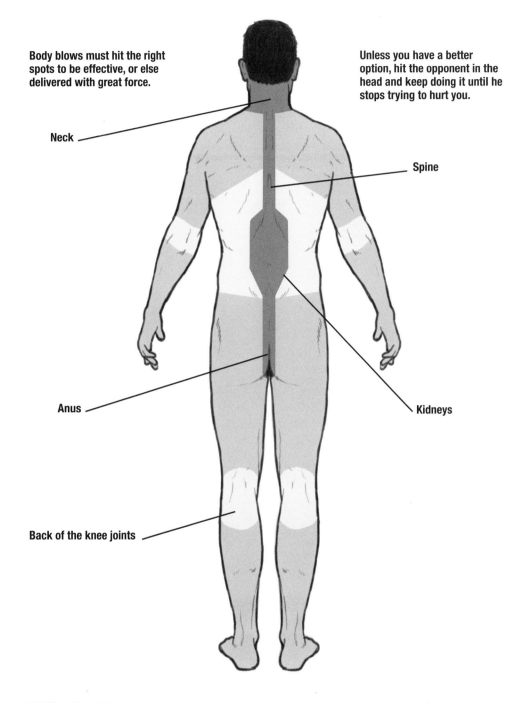

Body blows must hit the right spots to be effective, or else delivered with great force.

Unless you have a better option, hit the opponent in the head and keep doing it until he stops trying to hurt you.

Neck

Spine

Anus

Kidneys

Back of the knee joints

Hitting the Limbs

The limbs are not ideal targets for striking, although a 'dead leg' caused by kneeing the thigh can be very effective in limiting an opponent's movements. The shins are also surprisingly sensitive and can be kicked with a hard shoe to make the opponent flinch. Kicking the knee backwards or to the side can destroy the joint.

Effective Self-Defence

Any confrontation or violent situation is unpleasant and frightening, and there are no simple answers. Effective self-defence is a matter of playing the odds – increasing your own advantages and decreasing those of an opponent.

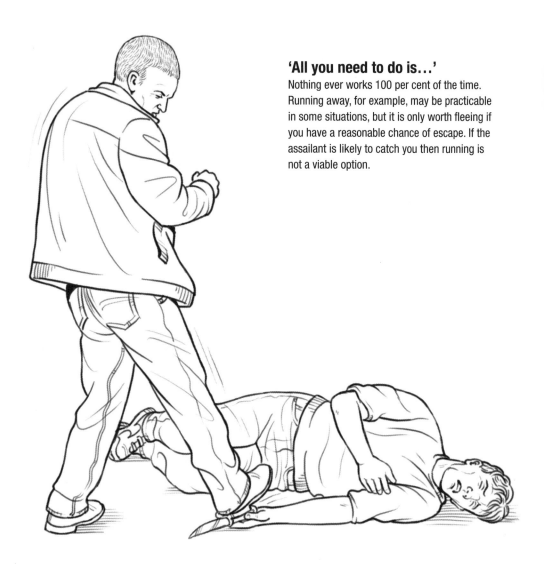

'All you need to do is…'

Nothing ever works 100 per cent of the time. Running away, for example, may be practicable in some situations, but it is only worth fleeing if you have a reasonable chance of escape. If the assailant is likely to catch you then running is not a viable option.

The Universal Rule

The only universal rule is that it is necessary to evaluate the situation – potential assailants, possible assistance, environmental factors and anything else that might affect the outcome – and formulate a response accordingly, i.e. you must fight smart and always keep in mind that the ultimate goal is your safety, which is not necessarily the same thing as winning a fight.

Simple answers like 'just kick him in the groin' are useless. You need a range of effective measures to cover all possibilities.

Dealing with Threats: Street Violence

Street fights tend to start suddenly (although an informed observer can usually see what is about to happen) and are usually short in duration. They are generally won by whoever lands the first clean blow to the head, and this is often the first punch. Usually this does not result in an instant knockout, and the rest of the 'fight' tends to be more of a beating delivered to someone who cannot properly defend himself.

The most common sort of attack, even with an assailant who has some training, is a barrage of extremely aggressive but not always very well executed punches. Some fights go to the ground, but most are already more or less won by this point. Your first priority must be to learn to fight standing up, since virtually all fights start this way.

Not all fights or physical assaults start with outright violence. There may be a confrontation, an exchange of threats and insults or other signs that things are going awry before punches are thrown. It may be possible to de-escalate a situation or withdraw from it at this stage, but once violence has begun it is usually necessary to use physical measures to end it.

The Fence Posture

The classic 'open hand' threat is an aggressive posture, 'pecking' with the head, arms spread wide to look bigger. It is usually accompanied by striding about, almost circling the victim, and shouting or snarling threats and abuse. Your fence should go up as soon as you see signs of aggression – even just an angry expression.

The Fence

The fence posture is in many ways quite similar to a combat stance, but it is fundamentally different in that it is a situation control tool, not a fighting stance. There are many variations on the theme, but the basic form of the fence is:

- Strong side back, weak side forward (i.e. left hand forward if you are right-handed)
- Feet about shoulder width apart
- Feet turned in and knees slightly flexed
- Appears casual and non-threatening, i.e. hands are open
- Places one or both hands as a physical and psychological barrier between you and the aggressor

The fence does not look aggressive in the way that a combat stance does, but it gives most of the same advantages. It allows free movement and rapid attack or defence, but does not give away your intentions. Most of all, it is designed to keep an aggressor at a distance.

If the aggressor is outside the fence, he cannot launch an attack from close range and is deprived of that advantage. From the security of your fence you can attempt to de-escalate the situation.

...If He Closes In

If an open-hand aggressor closes in and starts prodding or pushing it is obvious that he wants to escalate the confrontation. It may be possible to bring matters to a close by shoving him away and warning him to keep his distance, and it is probably worth trying this. Assertive action at this point may possibly prevent an attack, and if it happens then it would have happened anyway – but at least you have given yourself some space to react.

Combat Stance and Movement

A generic combat stance is not similar to the fence posture, other than being tighter and more obviously combat-orientated. Hands can be closed as fists or kept open to grab – whichever is natural to you will suffice. Weight is normally on the balls of your feet, allowing you to move quickly and lightly.

Weight is normally on the balls of your feet, allowing you to move quickly and lightly.

The 'Shuffle'

Use a 'shuffle' to move in a combat stance. Whichever foot is nearest the direction you want to go moves in that direction and the other pushes, then is brought up to put you back in your combat stance.

A good stance provides a firm
base to strike from, but still
retains good mobility.

A typical combat stance has the following characteristics:

- Strong side back, weak side forward (i.e. left hand forward if you are right-handed)
- Feet about shoulder width apart
- Feet turned in and knees slightly flexed
- Chin down to protect the jaw
- Elbows in to protect the ribs, hands fairly high to protect the head

The Punch Threat

In street fights, most aggressors tend to throw strong-hand power shots rather than fighting like a trained boxer. Since most people are right-handed, this means that the likely threat is a right-hand punch that will usually be a wild haymaker, or a grab with the weak hand and a straight punch with the right.

Headshots

Most assailants will swing at the head; it is rare to encounter body blows except at very close quarters. A big right will usually be followed by a big left, then another big right, although some assailants will bore in with repeated rights and largely forget about their left hand.

If you keep moving and guard your head with your hands you can make it very difficult for an aggressor to put you out of a fight.

Guard Your Head

A blow to the head that makes a clean connection can knock you out, send you reeling off balance or at least stun you. Even the most badly-executed haymaker can thus take you out of the fight or permit a follow-up blow to be landed. However, it is surprisingly difficult to make that clean connection if you are moving and have your hands up.

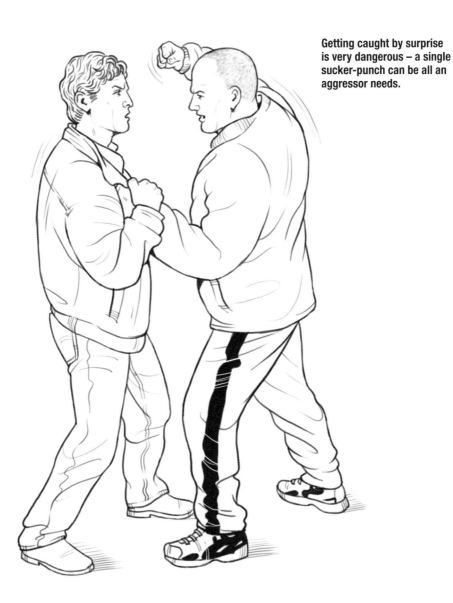

Getting caught by surprise is very dangerous – a single sucker-punch can be all an aggressor needs.

Dealing with Threats: Intimidation

Someone who is large and appears dangerous can intimidate an opponent to the point where they do not put up much of a fight, yet it might be that the victim could have won if they had tried. Physical factors such as size, strength and fighting ability are certainly important, but they are nothing if they are not driven by a will to win.

It is possible to successfully drive off an assailant by doing nothing more than making a lot of noise and ineffectually kicking and scratching. You must acknowledge that things are bad, but not hopeless. If you don't give up, then the only way to defeat you is to physically incapacitate you… and you can make that so difficult to do that the opponent gives up.

The Grab Threat

An assailant who grabs you will often try to drag you about, getting you physically and mentally off balance. Being slammed against a wall or furniture is as bad as being punched, and being pulled onto a blow will magnify its effects. Securing release from a grab is important, but it is not always your immediate concern. There is no point in fiddling about trying to release a grip on your lapel while being punched in the face.

Avoiding a Grab Attempt

If possible, avoid being grabbed by moving out of range, pre-empting the grab by striking the opponent or by batting his hands aside so that he cannot get a hold.

If the assailant has hold of your shirt with his left hand and is hitting you with his right, then the left is facilitating but the right is doing you harm. Deal with the blows, then free yourself.

A grab attempt should be viewed as every bit as serious as a blow, since it will make you very vulnerable to being struck.

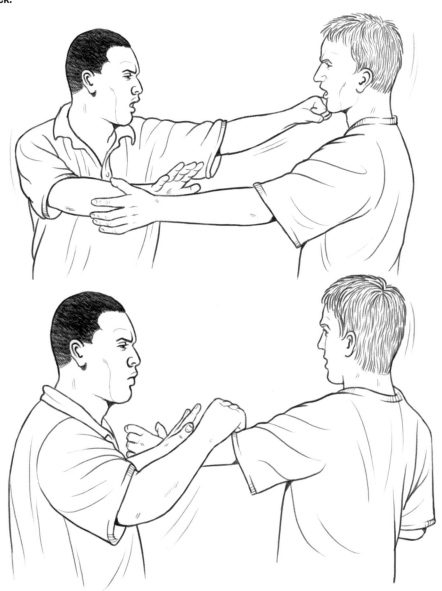

Escaping a Grab

Some grabs can be broken by twisting or jerking away, or by peeling the grabbing hand off you. If the grab is properly anchored you are unlikely to get free, even with the use of martial arts techniques. However, you can sometimes make the assailant want to let go by hurting him, or make it physically impossible to keep hold by breaking his fingers.

Pushing Techniques

Pushing someone is unlikely to end a confrontational situation, but it can be used to gain an advantage or to create space for an escape. From a fence position you might try to deter an aggressor by pushing him away and warning him to keep his distance, but you should only try this once. If he doesn't take the hint, he means business and a robust response is in order.

A push can be followed up with a psychological gambit, such as barking an order to leave you alone, or it can be used to make space for a strike.

One-Handed Pushing

A one-handed push is executed by placing your lead hand in the centre of the aggressor's sternum, with your arm slightly bent. Do not lean and push with a straight arm; instead you snap your arm straight and throw your weight into the push, driving the opponent sharply backwards.

Two-Handed Pushing

A two-handed push targets the shoulders of the aggressor, tipping him backwards with a sharp two-handed shove. Again, it is important to throw your weight into the push and to execute it sharply rather than leaning and pushing steadily.

You should never just turn and run away from someone who is right in front of you – you'll be caught. A push can make enough space to escape.

Be Aware of What's Around You

If you can shove someone away and get through a door that can be locked or jammed shut, then this is an effective escape. A barrier such as a table or shop counter can be used the same way as a fence posture. The opposite also applies – fleeing into a dead end or allowing yourself to become cornered can place you in grave danger.

It may be possible to break contact with an aggressor and hide, or to reach a place that is full of people. Do not forget that people, including the aggressor and anyone with him, are part of the environment. If you can push one opponent into another you might prevent both of them doing anything against you for a moment. If you can cause an aggressor to become entangled with bystanders, then this could put him out of the fight.

The environment can also be used directly against an opponent. Pushing is more effective if the opponent trips over something or is slammed into the edge of a table. A bag you are carrying can be tossed in front of a rushing aggressor. He may trip, but even if he does not you will have an opportunity to escape or strike him while he regains his equilibrium.

Defence Against a Straight Punch or Grab Attempt

The following defences are normally used in response to an attack, although it is possible to do something very similar in any situation where you find yourself in the same general position in relation to an opponent.

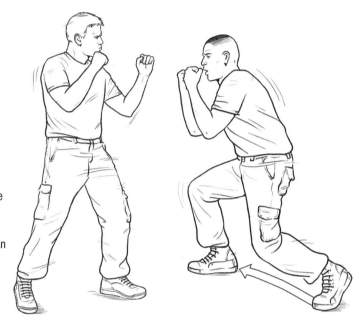

Evade and Counterattack

All of these defences involve stepping diagonally forward and to your right as the opponent moves in. They can be used against any attack that involves a straight arm. If the opponent gives you a straight right arm instead, you will need to go forward and left to evade the blow.

It is much easier to defend yourself when you are not immobilized by a grab, so wherever possible stay out of reach or knock any grab attempt away before it can be anchored in place.

The key is to get outside the arm and ensure that the grab or blow does not land, and then counterattack.

Deflect and Escape

If you can bat the strike or grab attempt to the side, it may be possible to simply break off and escape as the opponent tries to reorient himself. Alternatively, a counterpunch may be a good option, delivered as the opponent is off balance.

Evade and Arm Break

As the opponent reaches in or throws a straight punch, you move forward and diagonally to the right, stepping through with your rear foot (normally the right) and ending up facing the opponent while he is still facing the place where you were.

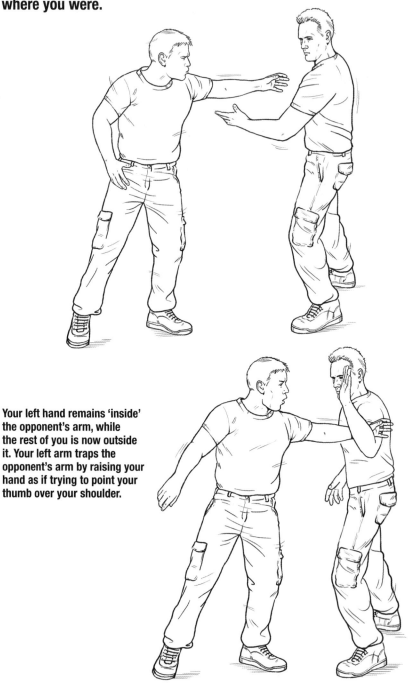

Your left hand remains 'inside' the opponent's arm, while the rest of you is now outside it. Your left arm traps the opponent's arm by raising your hand as if trying to point your thumb over your shoulder.

Drive forward with your right elbow, pushing it sharply through the opponent's trapped arm, and drive forward with the right hip as well. This forces his elbow against its range of motion and can break it.

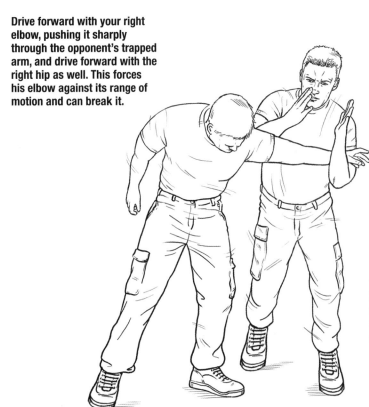

This position is used in a lot of control and restraint systems, and can be used to disarm an opponent if necessary.

Even if your counter does not break the aggressor's arm, you can get him under control by rotating to face the same direction he is and pushing down on his elbow and shoulder while pulling his arm upwards.

Tactical 'Y'

This move makes use of the 'tactical Y' concept. Moving up one of the arms of the Y will take you out of the threat zone.

Defence Against a Swinging Punch Attack

Big, swinging blows are relatively easy to see coming, which can be a mixed blessing. If you know what to do about a haymaker it can be fairly easy to defend against it, but many people will panic or freeze when they see the punch. It is possible to retreat out of range of a swinging punch but the aggressor will probably just follow you and throw more of them. The only viable answer is to defend in such a way as to set up your counter.

Cover and Control

A swinging punch can be effectively dealt with by covering the target area with your arm, using a movement much like answering a phone. Do not put your fist to your temple, but instead let your fingers go around the back of your head to anchor the cover in place. It is best to move forward, inside the arc of the swing, to weaken it. The punch will hit your cover and skid around the back, doing little harm.

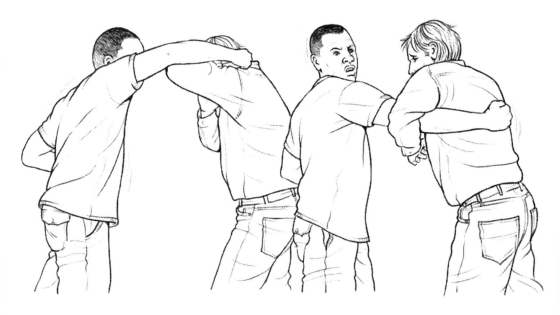

Control the Striking Arm

As soon as the blow strikes your arm, snake it around the attacker's arm and prevent him from withdrawing it for another blow. Your free hand can now be used to deliver short, hard blows to his face until he either struggles free or you let him go because he clearly does not want to fight any more.

The Commonest Threat

A swinging punch is by far the most likely attack you will face in a fight. Most inexpert swinging punches are badly aimed and do not connect cleanly even if the target stays still, but the aggressor will usually just keep swinging until he wins. Once you have been hit you may be stunned or taken off balance, leaving you vulnerable to additional blows.

Your cover can be made more effective by moving inside the arc of a swing, shortening and weakening it.

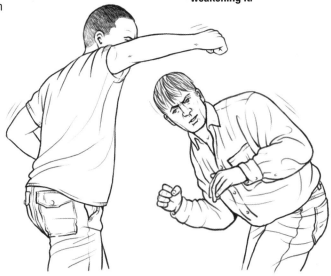

Alternative Counterattack

As an alternative, grab the aggressor around the back of the head with the hand you did not use for cover, and pull his head down and forward. This positions you to deliver repeated knee strikes to the body or the front of the legs.

Jam and Takedown

A swinging strike can be stopped by jamming it early in its progress. This works best with opponents who wind-up and throw large, clumsy strikes. Raise both arms so that your elbows point at the opponent and lunge forward, driving one elbow into the crook of his arm and one into his shoulder. This will be very painful for him, especially if he is throwing a powerful punch.

Drive forward to meet the strike and smother it. This not only stops the blow but also sets up a takedown that can win you the fight.

Take Him Down

As soon as you make contact, snake your outside arm around his striking arm and grip it tightly, using your other hand to push his head back and break his posture. Now step in close and hook his foot out from under him.

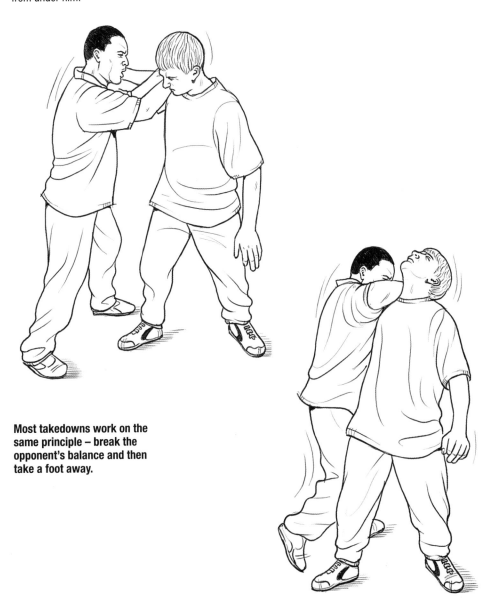

Most takedowns work on the same principle – break the opponent's balance and then take a foot away.

Head Over Heels

The key to this takedown is to get the opponent's head right back – past his heels – so that he is off balance, and only then to take away the foot. Done correctly it results in a very heavy fall.

Breaking a Wrist Hold

Wrist grabs are normally used to control someone while the aggressor does whatever he has in mind. This may be simply shouting at you, but the grab could equally be used to immobilize you while he strikes out, or to shake you around to disorient or unbalance.

Some aggressors will instinctively try to control your hands once a confrontation starts. This makes you very vulnerable and must be treated as an attack.

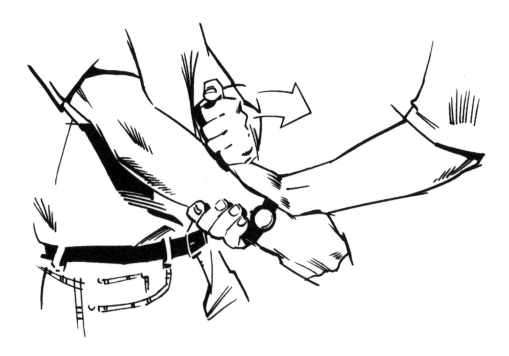

Break the Grip

The simplest way to escape a wrist grab is to twist the wrist and pull, using violent and jerky motions. The weakest part of the aggressor's grip is his thumb so you will want to pull the hand this way – trying to get out through the strongest part of the hand, the fingers, is unlikely to succeed. As an alternative, you can grab fingers or thumbs and wrench them, which will encourage the opponent to let go of you.

It is often possible to sharply twist your wrist free of a grab, especially if you act quickly before the grip is properly anchored.

The Grab Is Not the Whole Story

It is rare for an aggressor to get hold of a wrist and just stand there. He will usually be doing something else as well, so do not fixate on the wrist grip to the point where you are hit by a punch.

Close-Quarters Defence

Most fights that are not quickly ended by blows go to close quarters, with opponents grabbing at one another. Grabs are often used at the beginning of a fight or in a confrontation that has not yet quite become a fight. No matter why you are at close quarters, you need to deal with the situation fast. At such a short range there will be no time to react to whatever your opponent does next.

Grabs of any kind must be dislodged as quickly as possible, but this is not the end of the matter. You still have an aggressor right in your face who may hit you or get hold again. At the very least you will need to move sharply away or push the opponent from you, and if he seems very aggressive you would be well advised to strike him immediately in order to gain the initiative.

Strangles and Two-Handed Grabs

Introduction It is quite uncommon for an aggressor to begin an attack with a two-handed strangle attempt; it is typically used as a murderous finishing technique. Two-handed lapel grabs are more common, and are often used to set up a headbutt.

Break One Side

It may be possible to break one side of the grab or strangle by peeling one hand off you. This will make most strangles ineffective, but you need to take the initiative and fight your way out of the situation before the strangle hold can be re-established. One option is to loop your arm over the opponent's and push down against your chest, pulling his grip off you and trapping his hand.

Wedge Block

A two-handed grab can be dislodged with a 'wedge block', driving your hands close together and upwards between the opponent's arms. As your hands get higher, they spread further apart and push one or both of the opponent's hands off you. This is best followed up by a head grab and knee strikes.

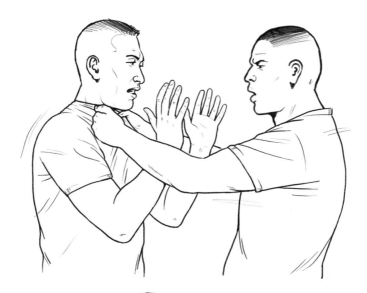

An aggressor who gets hold of your throat may strangle you without intending to. It is imperative to get the grip off your neck as fast as possible.

As with all grab attempts, you may be able to force the attacker to let go by attacking his head or by counterattacking with a knee hit.

Getting Out of Trouble

If you have been hit and are dazed, or when a barrage of blows is incoming and you have no time for a more thought-out response, then your best option is to 'crash in'. Cover your head with both arms, elbows pointing forward, and lunge at the opponent.

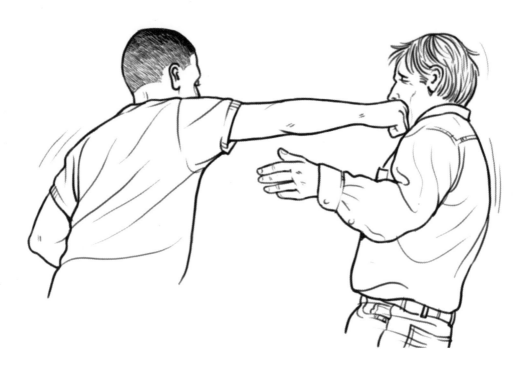

Offensive Defence

You have been caught unawares. The blows are raining in and you are not able to respond with counter punches or effective evasions. Firstly, move backwards out of immediate striking range. Then lunge forward, with your arms covering your head.

Crashing In

Your elbows will strike your opponent first, causing quite a lot of pain, and you will be protected by your arms from whatever he is doing. Once in close you may be able to trap his arm to stop him hitting you while you collect your wits and get back in the fight, or start delivering knee and elbow strikes.

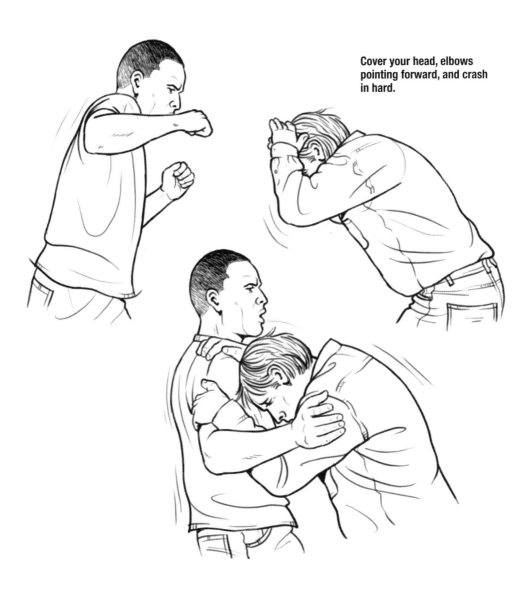

Cover your head, elbows pointing forward, and crash in hard.

Grab the opponent's arm and hang on, shutting down his strikes while you get back into the fight.

Pre-Emptive Hits

The ideal moment to strike an opponent is as he stands in front of you shouting threats, with his hands splayed to make himself look bigger and more threatening. Not only is this your best chance for a clean strike that will take him out of the fight, but hitting him while he thinks he is dominating the situation may well cause enough of a shock to make him want to escape rather than fight, defeating him psychologically.

It seems barbaric to strike the eyes, but if an aggressor intends to do you serious harm then this may be the only way to stop him.

Eye Jab Opener

From a fence stance, shoot your lead hand at the aggressor's eyes with the fingers slightly bent. This prevents damage if you hit his forehead. You can't burst an eyeball this way but you can make the opponent flinch, gaining time for a follow-up strike.

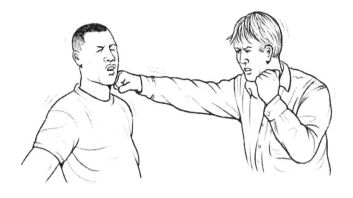

Good Mechanics

The cross is thrown from where your hand is, without a big wind-up, and travels in a straight line to the target's jaw. If you use a closed hand, a good tight fist is important to protect your hand from damage.

Keep Your Guard Up

If an opponent does not go down but seems to want to back off after you have hit him, keep your guard or fence up and do not taunt him – just let him go. If you insult or taunt him he may come back for another swing and you'll have to fight him all over again.

Palm-Heel Strike

Executed like a cross, a palm strike is often a better choice when hitting a hard target like the head. Bend your hand back as far as you can and keep the thumb out of the way to the side. The striking surface is the fleshy pad at the base of the hand, which transmits force well but protects the hand and wrist.

Elbow Strikes

Elbow strikes are excellent at close range and can be delivered with great force, even by a small and lightweight person. The elbow is very hard and will not be damaged by hitting a bony part of an opponent.

Twist It In

Body rotation is essential to develop sufficient force, and as with other strikes you must try to drive into and through the target rather than stopping or pulling the strike.

Just Like a Hook Punch

A hooking elbow is thrown much like a hooked punch, with your arm tucked out of the way so that your elbow contacts instead. Turn your hand so that your thumb is pointing down, as if you were looking at your watch.

Thrusting Elbow Strike

A thrusting elbow comes out to the side, although obviously you can turn to send the elbow wherever you want it to go. The strike is 'chambered' by drawing your arm across the body with the forearm parallel to the ground, and then delivered by thrusting it hard at the opponent. Leaning or stepping into the strike adds force.

A thrusting elbow can be used to intercept someone coming in to attack you from the side, or it can be delivered as you go past an assailant to escape from the situation.

Rear Elbow Strike

A similar thrusting elbow can be delivered to someone close behind, such as an assailant trying to grab you. This strike is chambered by pushing your hand out in front of you, palm up with the hand open or closed. It is delivered by simply slamming the arm backwards. It may be necessary to move slightly to the side in order to deliver a strike to an opponent directly behind you. A rear elbow can be made more powerful by twisting your body with the strike. A thrusting elbow lands harder if you either step into the strike or at least drive your shoulder into it.

Deflect and Body Blow

As the opponent reaches forward or tries to strike you, move diagonally forward, stepping through with the back foot. Instead of trapping his arm, your left hand (assuming he is attacking with his left) pushes the arm aside. Keeping your left hand on the opponent's left arm prevents him from turning to face you.

The important part of this technique is to deflect the strike or grab. Countering is secondary.

Body Shot

A body blow, such as a shovel hook, can be delivered from this position. Holding your fist just above the height of your waist, palm up, you are well positioned to drive it forward into the opponent's kidney area from the side or into his diaphragm, under the ribs.

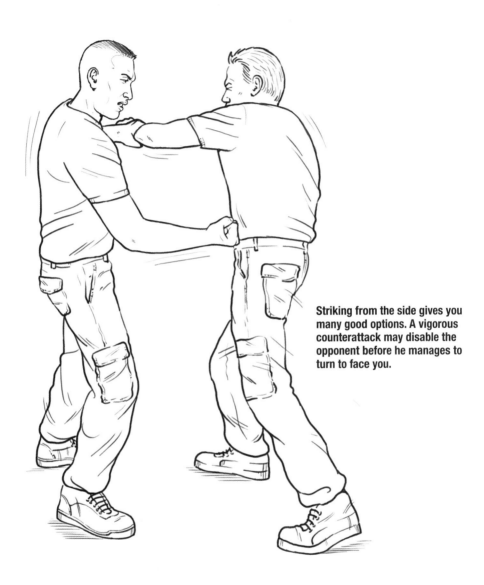

Striking from the side gives you many good options. A vigorous counterattack may disable the opponent before he manages to turn to face you.

Hard Weapon to Soft Target

A fist is the best tool for striking at softer areas of the body in this manner – it cannot be damaged and it focuses the impact to drive deep into the body.

Deflect and Elbow Strike

From the same position as the body blow, an excellent knockout can be achieved with a hooking elbow strike. This is executed by swinging the elbow in a short arc to strike the opponent behind the ear, driving his head forward and down. Even if he is not rendered unconscious he will be likely to stagger and may fall.

Control the Opponent

Normally the hand you have used to deflect or hold the opponent's arm remains in place to stop him turning to face you and your free arm delivers the strike, but this technique can be adapted to strike with either arm.

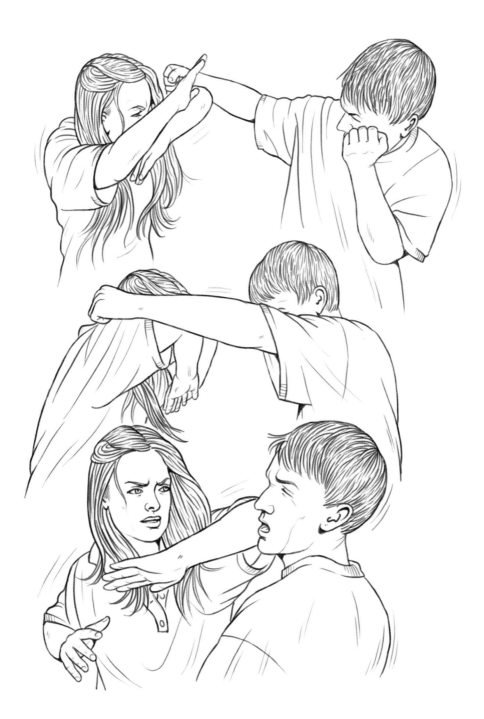

Cross-guard and Elbow Strike

The cross-guard is highy effective against hooked punches, as the opponent will tend to strike your elbows with his fists. The elbows should be held high in front of the head. The defender can turn defence into attack with a counterstrike if the opportunity allows.

Stomp Kick or Knee Strike

After evading out to the side as in the previous defences, you have some other good options. A knee strike can be delivered from the same position. Under the ribs is a good target to aim for as this will wind most people and make further aggressive action difficult.

Knee to the Leg

A knee driven hard into the side of the leg is also extremely effective. Even if it does not cause the leg to collapse it will make movement slow and painful, allowing a retreat or impairing the opponent's ability to fight if you need to finish the confrontation there and then.

It will be obvious whether you need to throw a straight or roundhouse knee strike from your position. Do what seems natural, and do it with conviction.

A stomp kick to the leg can cause permanent damage, but if it is your only chance to escape a beating or worse then it must be done.

Stomp Kick

Instead of pivoting to face the opponent, step forward so that you are alongside him facing in the opposite direction. Raise your foot and stomp downwards into the side of his knee. This can tear the knee joint apart and will disable the attacker for certain. However, the injury may well be permanent so this is a technique to be used only in the face of a fairly severe threat.

Clothing Grabs

It is possible that an aggressor might grab your lapel and just hang onto it, but it is likely that he intends to drag or hit you. A firmly anchored grab will not be readily dislodged by martial arts wristlocks. If the grab cannot be defeated by knocking it aside before it is anchored, the best option is to make the opponent want to let go.

Attack the Head

One option is to twist the opponent's wrist and hand outwards while either striking at his face or pushing his head back. This is done by putting the heel of your palm under his chin, fingers on his face, and tipping his head up and back. If you can get your fingers into his eyes he will usually be much more keen to let go and get out of reach.

One common street attack is to grab the lapel with the weak hand and strike with the strong one. Someone who grabs you with his left hand is almost certainly planning to punch with the right.

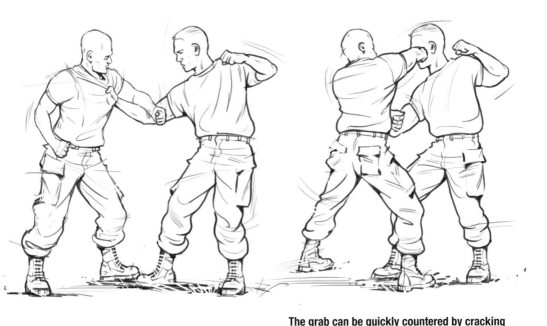

The grab can be quickly countered by cracking down hard with the forearm into the crook of the grabber's arm, driving down to pull the opponent forward, followed by a swift counterstrike.

Grab and Knee

Another option is to completely ignore the grab – the opponent has tied up one or both of his hands to no good effect – and lunge in, grabbing him around the neck. From here, start firing knee strikes at his body, groin and legs. He may well lose interest in keeping hold of you.

If You Get Knocked Down…

…try and get back on your feet as soon as you can. The first thing you need to do is prevent things getting any worse. As soon as you get the chance, get to your feet. You are vulnerable to being kicked while you are down.

Feet Towards the Enemy

Pivot to point your feet towards the assailant and kick out at his legs and knees if he tries to close in. A simple stamping action will keep most people at bay, and if you connect with his legs you may put him out of the fight.

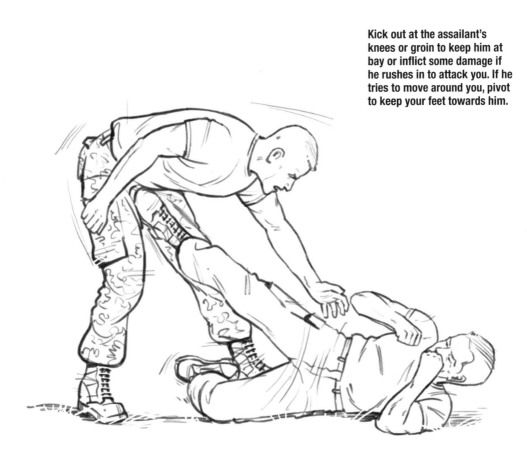

Kick out at the assailant's knees or groin to keep him at bay or inflict some damage if he rushes in to attack you. If he tries to move around you, pivot to keep your feet towards him.

Desperate Measures

Even if you are overmatched or obviously losing, you still have a chance while you keep fighting. Something as simple as struggling violently and making a lot of noise can sometimes drive off an opponent, who may fear intervention by others or decide that you are more trouble than you are worth.

Attacking the eyes, throat and face in general is always an option, as is biting. Unpleasant as it may be, you may be able to secure release from a grab by biting the hand that is holding you, or the opponent's face and body. Few people want to keep hold of someone who is determined to bite lumps off them.

As always, if you secure release or make your opponent recoil in horror then you need to exploit the advantage. This may mean following up with strikes or making a run for it, but either way you must do something or the opponent may renew his attack.

Final Notes

The ultimate goal in any self-defence scenario is to preserve your safety. If violence cannot be avoided then you must deal with it. If that means fighting until you win, so be it. If you can create an opportunity to escape or make your opponent reconsider his choice to attack you then that also works. Ultimately, it is all about preserving your safety by whatever means gives you the best chance of success. A very simple but useful set of self-defence rules looks like this:

- Strike with open hands, elbows or hammerfists to the head and with fists to the vulnerable areas of the body
- Strike with the knees to the body and the thigh
- Do not become involved in lengthy grappling or wrestling matches
- Avoid going to the ground if you possibly can
- If you cannot incapacitate an opponent, strikes can make some room for an escape
- Disengage and get away as soon as you can

Always remember the goal – it's not about 'winning a fight' or 'fighting back', it's about preserving your safety. If you can do that by withdrawing, talking or running then those are viable options. But if you have to fight, then you have to win.

Glossary

Choke: A choke constricts the windpipe and restricts the flow of air in and out of the body. It is accompanied by acute discomfort, which usually results in the victim struggling violently.

Elbow strikes: An elbow is much less likely to be injured than a fist if it strikes something hard. Elbow strikes include hooking elbows, which follow a more or less horizontal or overhand curved path, thrusting elbows, which are driven directly to the rear or side, and rising elbows, which come up under an opponent's chin.

Grappling: Any situation where the combatants are able to grab hold of one another. Most unarmed fights involve at least some grappling, though skilled fighters learn to use strikes as well as grappling moves when in close combat.

Kicks: Any strike with the foot or lower leg is a kick. A front kick comes directly out forwards; a roundhouse kick is a rotating kick normally thrown from the rear leg and impacts with the shin or instep.

Knee strikes: Any blow with the knee. A straight knee is usually delivered to the legs. A roundhouse knee follows a similar path to a roundhouse kick, and is often used against the opponent's ribs or abdomen.

Straight punch: Straight punches with the knuckles of a closed fist include the jab, which is a fast, light strike used mainly in boxing and similar competitions; the lead straight, which is similar but lands with much more force; and the cross, which is a very powerful blow delivered from the rear hand.

Strangle: A strangle cuts off the blood supply to the brain, resulting in rapid unconsciousness and, if kept in place, death. A firmly placed strangle can cause unconsciousness in a few seconds.

Takedown: A takedown is a technique designed to make an opponent fall or to drive him into the ground.